The real Deal

EATING RIGHT

Barbara Sheen

Heinemann
LIBRARY

www.heinemann.co.uk/library
Visit our website to find out more information about Heinemann Library books.

To order:

 Phone 44 (0) 1865 888112

 Send a fax to 44 (0) 1865 314091

Visit the Heinemann bookshop at www.heinemann.co.uk/library to browse our catalogue and order online.

First published in Great Britain by Heinemann Library, Halley Court, Jordan Hill, Oxford OX2 8EJ, part of Pearson Education.

Heinemann is a registered trademark of Pearson Education Ltd.

Editorial: Nancy Dickmann
Design: Richard Parker and Tinstar Design Ltd
Illustrations: Darren Lingard
Picture Research: Mica Brancic and Frances Topp
Production: Alison Parsons

Originated by Chroma Graphics
Printed and bound in China by Leo Paper Group

ISBN 978 0 431 90730 7 (hardback)
12 11 10 09 08

10 9 8 7 6 5 4 3 2 1

ISBN 978 0 431 90737 6 (paperback)
13 12 11 10 09

10 9 8 7 6 5 4 3 2 1

British Library Cataloguing in Publication Data
Sheen, Barbara.
   Eating right. - (The real deal)
   1. Nutrition - Juvenile literature
   I. Title
   613.2

A full catalogue record for this book is available from the British Library.

Acknowledgments
The publishers would like to thank the following for permission to reproduce photographs: Action Images/ John Marsh/Livepic p. **4**; Alamy pp. **10** (don jon red), **12** (StockAB), **13** (Chuck Pefley), **23** (mediacolor's); Anthony Blake pp. **5**, **16**; Art Directors/Helene Rogers p. **21**; Corbis pp. **20** (zefa/H. Schmid), **24** (Image Source); Getty/Stone/Christopher Bissell p. **15**; Getty Images News/Chris Jackson p. **18**; PhotoLibrary pp. **22** (Creatas), **27** (Radius Images); Science Photo Library/ Mauro Fermariello p. **25**; SuperStock pp. **7** (Mauritius), **9** (Francisco Cruz), **14**, **17**, **19** (age fotostock); US Department of Agriculture p. **11**.

Cover photograph of an arrow road sign reproduced with permission of iStockphoto/Nicholas Belton; cover photographs of a strawberry and an orange slice reproduced with permission of Getty Images/ PhotoDisc.

The publishers would like to thank Dr. Sarah Schenker for her assistance in the preparation of this book.

Every effort has been made to contact copyright holders of any material reproduced in this book. Any omissions will be rectified in subsequent printings if notice is given to the publishers.

Contents

Some words are shown in bold, **like this**. You can find out what they mean by looking in the glossary.

Valuable nutrients

The human body is amazing and complex. Like a race car, it needs fuel to run. A race car's fuel is petrol, while the human body's fuel is food. Food supplies the body with **nutrients,** the natural substances that keep the body working properly. Nutrients are organized into six groups: **proteins**, **fats**, **carbohydrates**, **vitamins**, **minerals**, and water.

Each nutrient has a different job. To stay healthy, each person needs to get enough of each nutrient every day. Not getting enough of a nutrient, or getting too much of some nutrients, can affect a person's health.

Foods that are loaded with nutrients are **nutrient dense** foods. However, no single food contains every nutrient. The only way for people to get all the nutrients they need is by eating a variety of nutrient dense foods every day.

Like any machine, the body needs fuel to power it.

Proteins

The human body is made up of proteins. Smaller units called **amino acids** are the building blocks of proteins. They replace and repair the millions of **cells** that make up the body.

Meat, fish, poultry, eggs, milk, and soya beans contain different proteins. Because they have all the essential amino acids, they are complete proteins. Dried beans, corn, wheat, nuts, seeds, and rice also contain protein, but not the amino acids essential for cell-building.

A balanced diet made up of a variety of nutrient dense foods fuels the body.

Top Tip

Complete proteins tend to come from animal products, but **vegetarians** can still get all the protein they need by combining plant proteins. For example, combining peanut butter and wholewheat bread will supply all of the essential amino acids the body needs.

Type of fat	Main source
Monounsaturated	Olive, canola, and peanut oils; olives; avocados; cashews, almonds, peanuts, and most other nuts
Polyunsaturated	Fish, nuts, grains
Saturated	Whole milk, butter, cheese, and ice cream; chocolate; red meat; coconuts, coconut milk, and coconut oil
Trans fatty acids	Most margarines; vegetable shortening; partially hydrogenated vegetable oil; many fast foods; most commercial baked goods

Monounsaturated and polyunsaturated fats help to keep blood cholesterol levels healthy.

Fats

The body gets energy from fats. Fats also insulate the body and help keep it warm. In addition, fats help the body to **absorb** some vitamins. The body needs some fats from the diet, but eating too much fat can be unhealthy.

There are three kinds of fats: saturated, unsaturated, and **trans fatty acids** (often called "trans fats"). Trans fats and **saturated fats** are solid at room temperature. Eating too many can raise levels of cholesterol in the blood. This can clog **blood vessels** and cause heart disease.

Meat and milk products contain saturated fats. Trans fats are found in **processed foods** such as crisps, pastries, and some margarines. Eating too many trans fats and saturated fats can cause diseases such as heart disease, stroke, cancer, **diabetes**, high blood pressure, and obesity. Obesity is a disorder in which people have more body fat than is healthy.

Unsaturated fats are liquid at room temperature. There are two types. Monounsaturated fats are found in certain oils, such as olive oil and peanut oil. Polyunsaturated fats are found in nuts, grains, and fish. Unsaturated fats help to keep blood cholesterol levels healthy.

Carbohydrates

Energy also comes from carbohydrates. They come in two varieties – simple and complex. Many foods that contain complex carbohydrates are nutrient dense. The body breaks them down slowly, so they give the body long-lasting energy. Potatoes, dried beans, pasta, and **whole grains** are rich in complex carbohydrates.

Sugary foods contain simple carbohydrates and few other nutrients. Eating too many simple carbohydrates can cause problems. Eating too many sugary foods increases the risk of tooth cavities. Eating large amounts of **non-nutrient dense** foods is also linked to obesity.

Top Tip

Sugar-rich foods such as sweets and soft drinks contain simple carbohydrates. The body breaks simple carbohydrates down quickly. They give the body a short burst of energy. For energy that lasts, eat complex carbohydrates, which break down more slowly.

Whole grains contain fibre and complex carbohydrates.

Vitamins

The body only needs small amounts of vitamins, but without them it would not work properly. Fruits, vegetables, milk, whole grains, nuts, beans, meats, and seafood are full of the vitamins the body needs.

The main vitamins are A, C, D, E, and K. The vitamin B family is also important, including vitamins B_6, B_{12}, thiamine, riboflavin, niacin, folic acid, and pantothenic acid. Vitamin A helps people see, especially at night. It may help fight infection, along with vitamin C. The B vitamins help the body get energy from food. Vitamin K helps the blood to clot.

We need a certain amount of each vitamin every day. Amounts of some vitamins, such as D, E, and K, are stored in the body. Vitamins C and B cannot be stored in the body. They must be replaced completely every day.

Vitamins and minerals have many important jobs.

Vitamin or mineral	What it does	Where to find it
Calcium	Helps build strong teeth and bones; helps blood clot	Dairy products, sardines, broccoli, and other dark green vegetables
Iron	Helps blood production	Liver, red meat, whole grains, shellfish, dark green vegetables
Potassium	Helps the nerves and heart	Oranges, bananas, meat, fish, potatoes, beans, cereal
Vitamin A	Helps keep eyes, skin, and hair healthy	Milk, butter, cheese, eggs, liver
Vitamin B_6	Important for the nervous system and blood production	Meat, vegetables, nuts, beans, fish, rice, yeast
Vitamin C	Helps build strong gums, teeth, and bones	Oranges and other citrus fruits, berries, peppers, cabbage
Vitamin D	Helps build strong teeth and bones	Milk, eggs, salmon, tuna, cod liver oil
Vitamin E	Helps blood production	Vegetable oil, grains
Zinc	Helps wounds heal	Meat, whole grains, milk, beans

Vitamins and minerals help maintain a strong body and help people get energy from food.

Minerals

The human body depends on 16 different minerals. Zinc helps fight infection. Calcium, magnesium, and phosphorus keep bones strong. Iron helps carry oxygen through the body. Potassium and sodium keep muscles working well, especially the heart. Citrus fruits, nuts, and bananas are high in potassium, while milk and yoghurt are good sources of calcium.

As with other nutrients, too many or two few minerals can be a problem. For example, too much sodium or salt, combined with too little potassium and calcium, may cause high blood pressure.

Water

Water is essential to a healthy body. The human body needs water to digest food and remove waste. People should aim to drink eight to twelve glasses of water per day.

Taking responsibility

Each person needs to take responsibility for his or her own health. Eating a variety of nutrient dense foods is a key step to staying healthy. Sometimes it is hard to know which foods to choose and how much of them to eat.

The Balance of Good Health

The government has created a tool to help people make healthy food choices. The **Balance of Good Health** is made up of five different coloured sections. Each section stands for a **food group.** The bigger the section, the more food from its group a person needs to eat each day.

Making food choices can be confusing.

Eating a balance of foods from different food groups is the key to a healthy diet.

In order to have a healthy diet we need to eat something from the four biggest sections each day. This will make sure that we get the wide range of nutrients our bodies need to help them stay healthy. The fifth and smallest section has foods containing fat and sugar. It is okay to eat these foods, but they should not be eaten very often and only in small amounts.

The Balance of Good Health does not recommend how much food a person should eat. This is because different people need to eat different amounts in order to stay healthy. The important thing is getting the right balance from the different food groups.

Top Tip

You should eat at least five portions of fruit and vegetables every day. An apple, orange, or banana is one portion. So is half a tablespoon of dried fruit, two to three tablespoons of vegetables, or one glass (150 ml) of fruit juice. Your portion can be fresh, frozen, chilled, or canned. It can be eaten on its own or as part of another food, such as a stew or soup.

Food labels

In the United Kingdom, all packaged food must have a food label. Some food labels contain nutritional facts. These facts can help people to make healthy food choices.

When nutritional information is given on a label it must include energy, protein, carbohydrates, and fat. The food label must say how much of each of these nutrients can be found in 100g or 100ml of the food. Sometimes the label will also tell you how much of each nutrient you get in one serving of the food.

What do you think?

Schools are now banning the serving of sweets, crisps, and fizzy drinks at lunch. Some people think that banning these foods will help keep pupils healthy. Other people disagree with this. They say that individuals and families should make their own food decisions. What do you think?

All food labels must show the nutrients that the food contains.

INGREDIENTS

Wheat, Brown Sugar, Glucose Syrup, Honey (3%), Niacin, Iron, Riboflavin (B2), Thiamin (B1).

NUTRITION INFORMATION

Typical Values	per 100g	per 30g serving
Energy	1620kJ (387 kcal)	486kJ (116 kcal)
Protein	6.5g	2.0g
Carbohydrate	86.5g	26.0g
(of which sugars)	49.0g	14.7g
Fat	1.0g	0.3g
(of which saturates)	0.2g	0.06g
Fibre	3.0g	0.9g
Sodium	trace	trace

Vitamins & Mineral

	per 100g	per 30g serving
Thiamin (B1)	1.0mg/71% RDA*	0.3mg/21%RDA*
Riboflavin (B2)	1.0mg/63% RDA*	0.3mg/19%RDA*
Niacin	10mg/56% RDA*	3.0mg/17%RDA*
Iron	8.0mg/57% RDA*	2.4mg/17%RDA*

Thiamin (B1)	Essential for growth and for the release of energy from carbohydrate
Riboflavin (B2)	Essential for growth, for the release of energy from carbohydrate and the maintenance of healthy skin and eyes
Niacin	Essential for the release of energy from food and the maintenance of healthy skin, and digestive and nervous systems
Iron	Essential for the body's use of oxygen, carrying it to all the cells of the body

*RDA = Recommended daily allowance

The amount of energy in a food is measured in joules (kJ) or **calories** (kcal). Other nutrients are measured in grams (g) and milligrams (mg). Some labels also show percentages (%). The percentages are based on GDAs (guideline daily amounts), sometimes called RDAs (recommended daily allowances). This is the amount of the nutrient that an adult should get each day. An adult usually needs more of each nutrient than a child does.

Some shops are now using the traffic light system of labelling. This tells you at a glance the amount of fat, salt, and added sugar there is in a food. Red is high, amber is medium, and green is low. Because these are things we should try to avoid for a healthy diet, the more greens on a label the better the food is for you.

One eclair provides...
cal 218
fat 16.0g
sat fat 8.2g
salt 0.3g
total sugars 10.5g

The traffic light system of labelling makes it quick and easy for shoppers to find healthy foods.

Advertising and food choices

Advertising can play a role in food choices. Food adverts try to make people buy a particular brand of food. They make food look appealing, but rarely tell us its nutritional value.

In recent times, advertisers spent around £40 million each year marketing food to children. Cartoon characters and celebrities were used to advertise non-nutrient dense foods. Food adverts would also show people having fun. Adverts like this make people think that if they eat the advertised food, they will have fun too.

Some experts say that these ads are one reason why one in five British children are overweight or **obese.** New laws were introduced in April 2007 to stop this kind of advertising. Before this, nearly one hundred percent of food adverts during children's programmes were for non-nutrient dense foods.

Some foods, such as chips, are advertised in a way that makes them attractive to young people.

Peer pressure

Peers can also influence what we eat. **Peer pressure** is pressure put on a person by others to behave in a certain way. Peer pressure causes people to do things they might not otherwise do. They do these things to be liked or fit into a group. For example, if a group of young people eats junk food at lunch, other young people may do the same thing just to fit in.

Being responsible

Being responsible means making responsible choices. Peer pressure can be very powerful. So can adverts. That is why it is important to think before eating a food. Does it give you the nutrients you need? Do you really want to eat it or do friends or adverts influence your choice?

Friends can influence each other's food choices.

Case Study

Not getting enough minerals causes problems. Rob was always tired. A blood test showed that Rob did not have enough red blood cells. These cells carry oxygen to the rest of the body. Rob needed to eat more iron. He added more iron-rich foods such as red meat, **whole grains**, and eggs to his diet. Soon he was feeling better.

How much food is enough?

There is no simple answer to this question. Eating larger or smaller **portions** than necessary can affect a person's body, but proper portion size varies from person to person. Active people need more energy to fuel their bodies than inactive people. A person's age, height, and weight also affect the amount of food he or she needs.

No matter how much people eat they still may not get all the nutrients they need. Eating a lot of non-nutrient dense foods, such as sweets, provides energy but does not supply many nutrients. People need to eat a balance of nutrients to be healthy. This means that people need to get most of their energy from a variety of nutrient dense foods.

NEWSFLASH

According to experts, one-fifth of boys and one-third of girls in the UK will be obese by the year 2020. By 2025 nearly half of all children in Australia will be overweight or obese. Cases of type 2 diabetes, a disease linked to being overweight, is also on the rise in young people.

Many foods add energy without providing a variety of important nutrients.

Being active burns energy and helps prevent obesity. Playing volleyball for an hour burns about 1197 kJ.

Overeating

When people eat more food than their bodies can use, the extra energy is changed to fat. The fat is stored in their body. As more fat is stored, people gain weight. Extra fat can make a person become overweight or obese. These conditions increase a person's chances of heart disease, diabetes, cancer, arthritis, and high blood pressure. In fact, 90 percent of people with type 2 diabetes, an incurable disease, and about one-third of people with high blood pressure are overweight or obese.

Top Tip

A 45.35-kilogram (100-pound) person burns about 200 kJ (48 kcal) per hour, even just sitting still. Being active burns even more.

Walking moderately	665 kJ
Dancing	1140 kJ
Skating	1330 kJ
Bicycling moderately	1520 kJ
Running five miles per hour	1520 kJ
Playing football	1900 kJ
Skipping	1900 kJ
Swimming laps	1900 kJ

Undereating

When people undereat, they take in less energy than their bodies need. This causes their bodies to burn muscle tissue and stored fat for energy, which leads to weakness and poor health.

Over time, undereating can cause **malnutrition,** a condition in which the body does not get enough nutrients. A lack of certain vitamins is one symptom of malnutrition. This can cause serious health problems. Severe malnutrition can cause death.

Why do people overeat and undereat?

Many people have no choice about undereating. They cannot afford enough food to keep them healthy. People who do not have problems getting food often undereat to lose weight. They should only do this with the help of a doctor or a registered **dietitian.** That way they can be sure they are still getting all the nutrients they need.

Food shortages lead to malnutrition, and can cause people to starve to death.

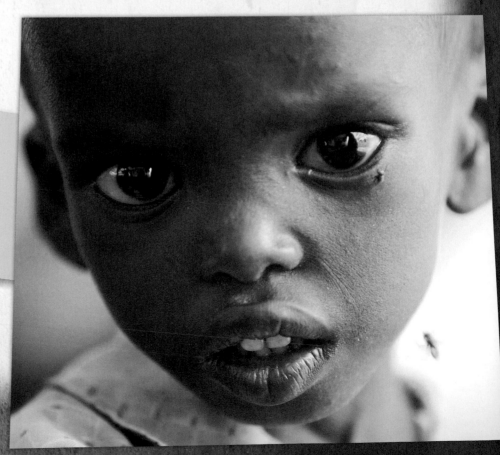

When people feel lonely or bored, doing a hobby can keep their minds off eating.

Some people undereat for emotional reasons. **Depression** or **stress** causes them to lose their appetite. To be healthy, these people must eat even when they are feeling upset. Depression and stress can cause other people to overeat. So can loneliness and boredom. Food gives some people comfort. It fills an emptiness they feel. People who are emotional eaters should see their doctor or a registered dietitian for advice.

Dealing with emotional issues helps people change their eating behaviours. Substituting pleasant activities such as a hobby or a physical activity for overeating may help too. Seeing a doctor or a registered dietitian also helps people maintain proper eating habits.

Top Tip

Not getting enough vitamins can cause problems. For example, a vitamin A deficiency causes vision problems. Deficiencies of some B vitamins cause weak muscles and skin problems. A vitamin C deficiency causes a disease called scurvy. It also makes it hard to fight infection. A vitamin D deficiency causes weak bones and rickets, a bone disease.

Self-esteem and eating disorders

Low **self-esteem** can cause people to overeat or undereat. Low self-esteem can make people feel they are unattractive. They may become so keen on losing weight that they develop an eating disorder such as **anorexia** or **bulimia.** People with anorexia refuse to eat. Those with bulimia eat normally, but take unusual steps to eliminate food from their bodies. They may make themselves vomit, or take laxatives, or over-exercise.

Obesity is another eating disorder. In this case, low self-esteem and emotions cause people to overeat. Eating disorders can cause death if not treated. Seeing a doctor can help.

Loneliness or other emotional problems can lead to eating disorders.

Case Study

Jessica was obese. Because she was lonely, she overate. She attended a summer camp for children with eating disorders. She learned healthier ways to deal with her feelings. Special camps are just one of the many ways people with eating disorders can get help.

How much?

One way to know how much to eat is think about the amount of energy you get from food. Different people have different energy needs. Their needs depend on their height and weight, as well as how active they are. No matter how much or how little a person eats, the balance of food groups is always important.

When people think about their energy intake, it is important for them to consider the balance of nutrients as well. The amount of energy in a food is not the same as the amount of nutrients. For example, both a banana and 28 grams (1 ounce) of jellybeans each contain the same amount of energy – about 440 kJ (105 kcals). However, the banana also contains protein, complex carbohydrates, fibre, vitamins, and minerals. The jellybeans contain only simple carbohydrates. The banana gives the body more of what it needs. Most nutrient dense foods do the same.

Both of these have about the same amount of energy, but the nuts also contain protein, fibre, vitamins, and minerals.

Putting it all together

Eating healthily can be confusing. It is like putting together a large jigsaw puzzle. It is not easy, but when all the pieces fit, you get a picture of a healthy person.

All foods can fit into a healthy diet. Eating the right amounts of each type of nutrient is the key. Eating mainly non-nutrient dense foods is unhealthy, as is eating foods from just one food group. People need to eat a wide variety of foods to get all the nutrients they need. Non-nutrient dense foods should not make up the main part of a person's diet, but eating a small amount is fine.

As long as people eat mainly nutrient dense foods, all foods can fit into a healthy diet.

NEWSFLASH

The size of containers, plates, and utensils affects how much people eat. In a study from 2006, scientists found that doubling the size of the bowls increased the amount of ice cream people ate by 31 percent.

Eating five servings of colourful fruits and vegetables every day promotes good health.

Eating sensible sized portions helps keep people healthy. For example, many fast food and other restaurants offer super-sized portions. But a small order of chips will help satisfy a hunger for chips and still leaves room for more nutrient dense foods. Sharing a sweet dessert after a nutrient dense meal is also a good way to enjoy a favourite food and eat in balance.

Top Tip

When we eat, colour counts. Brightly coloured fruits and vegetables contain phyto-nutrients, plant substances that improve health. Fruits and vegetables that are blue, purple, and red look after your heart. Green ones build strong bones and teeth and promote good vision. Yellow and orange fight infection and help prevent heart disease. All fruits and vegetables help prevent cancer.

Healthy choices

Everyone's day should start with breakfast. People use energy even when they sleep. When people get up in the morning, their bodies have gone without food for many hours. They need food to refuel their body. Without breakfast, people feel tired. Eating breakfast energizes a person's body. Breakfast also keeps people from overeating during the rest of the day.

Eating a doughnut that contains simple carbohydrates for breakfast will get you going, but not for long. A bowl of porridge topped with milk, nuts, and fruit contains complex carbohydrates, protein, vitamins, and minerals. It provides lasting energy.

You do not have to eat a traditional breakfast to get a good start. Any variety of nutrient-rich foods can be eaten for breakfast. A glass of milk and a peanut butter and banana sandwich is a great way to start the day. So is yoghurt with fruit and nuts.

NEWSFLASH

Eating breakfast helps students to be more alert. Studies have shown that students who eat breakfast do better in tests than those who do not eat breakfast. They can work longer, have fewer behavioural problems, and are absent less often than students who skip breakfast.

Pupils who skip breakfast find it harder to concentrate.

Lunch

Many people eat lunch at school or work. Packed lunches can be delicious and nutrient dense. A turkey sandwich topped with lettuce on a whole grain roll with milk and a cupful of fresh fruit is a tasty, nutrient dense lunch. A thermos-full of bean soup or meat stew accompanied by a stick of low-fat mozzarella cheese, a piece of wholemeal pitta bread, and an apple is another nutrient dense choice.

Making healthy lunch choices will help our bodies to get a variety of nutrients. Eating non-nutrient dense foods may make you full, but they do not provide the nutrients you need.

This delicious lunch is loaded with nutrients.

Dinner

Dinner is a good time for families to gather and share a variety of foods. Pasta topped with tomato sauce and grilled chicken, a green vegetable, and a glass of milk is a tasty, balanced dinner. A juicy pear or other fruit is a healthy dessert. Vegetarians might enjoy a black bean burger on a whole grain bun. Topping it with lettuce and tomato adds vitamins and minerals. A baked potato and a glass of milk are nutrient dense side dishes. For dessert, why not try a scoop of fat-free frozen yoghurt topped with berries?

Snacks

Healthy snacking keeps a person's body fuelled. However, regular snacking on non-nutrient dense foods such as sweets causes feelings of low energy. Simple carbohydrates cause blood sugar levels to rise sharply and then drop. This makes people feel tired, and they will need to eat again to raise their energy level.

At home or in a restaurant, think about how much you eat.

Food	Average serving size	How big is it?
Chicken	1 breast (85 grams)	about the size of a deck of cards
Apple	1 medium	about the size of a light bulb
Cheese	56 grams	about the size of a domino
Pasta	1 cup	about the size of a tennis ball

A tasty snack of plain popcorn provides long-lasting energy and fibre.

Snacks such as a hard-boiled egg, yoghurt, and nuts provide protein and long-lasting fuel. Fresh fruits and vegetables provide energy, vitamins, minerals, and fibre. Dipping them in cottage cheese or hummus adds protein.

Drinks

Water is the healthiest beverage choice. Drinking plenty of water keeps a body working. Nutrient dense beverages such as real fruit juices are also delicious snacks. Milk and milkshakes made with real fruit and lowfat milk provide energy and help strengthen bones. Nutrient dense drinks help keep us healthy and taste delicious.

Top Tips

Make healthy choices when eating at a restaurant by thinking about how the food you order is prepared. Is it roasted, grilled, or fried? You can also think about the balance of nutrients on your plate. Side orders such as salads or mixed fruit can help you achieve your five portions a day.

Nutrient chart

Nutrient	Where can I find it?	What does it do?
Protein	Fish, chicken, beef, pork, eggs, milk, cheese, yogurt, rice, dried beans, peas, lentils, nuts, seeds, wheat, oats, and corn all contain protein.	Almost all the parts of our bodies are made from protein. It helps cells to grow and repairs or replaces healthy cells and tissues.
Carbohydrates	Cereals, bread, rice, pasta, potatoes, corn, berries, oranges, and apples all contain carbohydrates. So do many other foods.	Carbohydrates are the body's main source of energy.
Fats	Fat is found in many foods, such as meat and dairy products. We often add fats such as butter, oil, or margarine to foods. Snacks, pastries, and prepared foods often contain fat.	Fat is an important source of energy. Fat also helps carry and store some types of vitamins, such as vitamins A and D.
Vitamins	There are many different types of vitamins, and they are found in different foods. Meat, milk, eggs, fish, whole grains, beans, nuts, green vegetables, and fruit are all good sources of vitamins.	Vitamins have different jobs. Some of them help your body use the energy you get from food. Others help the body build new cells. We need to get enough of some vitamins in order to prevent disease.
Minerals	Different minerals are found in different foods. Meats, whole grains, milk, green vegetables, fruit, beans, cereal, potatoes, seafood, and cheese all contain minerals.	Minerals have different jobs. Calcium helps keep teeth and bones strong, while iron helps form blood cells. Other minerals play a part in healing wounds, helping our nerves, and much more.

How much energy?

Making healthy food choices can be confusing. This chart shows some common foods and the amount of energy they contain. But remember, energy is only part of the picture. Read food labels carefully and see which nutrients each food contains.

Type of food	Average serving	Energy
Apple	1 medium	523 kJ (125 kcal)
Bagel (plain)	1	837 kJ (200 kcal)
Banana	1 medium	440 kJ (105 kcal)
Beefburger	1	1026 kJ (245 kcal)
Broccoli, cooked	156g (1 cup)	230 kJ (55 kcal)
Carrot	1 medium	126 kJ (30 kcal)
Cheddar cheese	28g (1 oz)	481 kJ (115 kcal)
Chicken noodle soup	237 ml (1 cup)	314 kJ (75 kcal)
Chicken breast, roasted	85g (3 oz)	586 kJ (140 kcal)
Chocolate chip cookies	4 cookies	754 kJ (180 kcal)
Cola, regular	355 ml (12 fl oz)	670 kJ (160 kcal)
Corn flakes	28g (1 oz)	461 kJ (110 kcal)
Crisps	10 crisps	440 kJ (105 kcal)
Egg, hard-boiled	1 egg	314 kJ (75 kcal)
Ice cream (chocolate)	132g (1 cup)	1193 kJ (285 kcal)
Milk, lowfat (1%)	237 ml (1 cup)	419 kJ (100 kcal)
Orange juice	237 ml (1 cup)	461 kJ (110 kcal)
Peanut butter	11g (1 tbsp)	398 kJ (95 kcal)
Pizza, plain cheese	1 slice	1214 kJ (290 kcal)
Popcorn, air-popped	8g (1 cup)	126 kJ (30 kcal)
Porridge	80g (1 cup)	607 kJ (145 kcal)
Potato, baked	1 medium	921 kJ (220 kcal)
Rice, cooked	158g (1 cup)	858 kJ (205 kcal)
Tomato soup	237 ml (1 cup)	356 kJ (85 kcal)
Tuna	85g (3 oz)	565 kJ (135 kcal)
Wholewheat bread	1 slice	293 kJ (70 kcal)

Glossary

absorb take in or soak up

amino acid substance that makes up proteins

anorexia eating disorder in which people starve themselves

Balance of Good Health tool that shows recommended daily food choices

blood vessel tube in the body that carries blood to tissues and organs

bulimia eating disorder in which people eliminate food by using laxatives, vomiting, or over-exercising

calorie measure of the amount of energy in food

carbohydrate essential nutrient that gives the body energy

cell basic unit of life

diabetes incurable disease in which blood sugar levels are higher than normal

dietitian person who is an expert in diet and nutrition

depression ongoing feeling of sadness

fat essential nutrient that gives the body heat and energy

fibre part of fruits, vegetables, grains, nuts, seeds, and beans that the body cannot digest

food group way to classify foods

grain seed and fruit of plants such as wheat, corn, rice, barley, and rye

malnutrition condition in which the body does not get enough essential nutrients

mineral essential nutrient such as calcium, iron, magnesium, and potassium

non-nutrient dense containing few nutrients

nutrient substance in food that helps the body to grow and function

nutrient dense containing many nutrients

obese being more than 20 percent above normal body weight

peer pressure social pressure to behave or look a certain way in order to be accepted by a group

portion serving size

processed food food that contains chemicals and preservatives

protein essential nutrient that is needed for cell repair

saturated fat fat that is solid at room temperature

self-esteem respect for self

stress pressure

trans fatty acid human-made fat found in processed food

unsaturated fat fat that is liquid at room temperature

vegetarian person who does not eat meat products

vitamin essential nutrient that the body needs to be healthy

whole grain grain that has not had any part removed

Further Resources

Books

Eating (My amazing body), Angela Royston (Raintree, 2004)

Eating Properly (It's your health!), Jonathan Rees (Watts, 2004)

Food for Feeling Healthy, Carol Ballard (Heinemann Library, 2007)

Websites

Food Standards Agency
www.eatwell.gov.uk

School Food Trust
www.schoolfoodtrust.org.uk

What's Inside Guide
www.whatsinsideguide.com/spreadingtheword.aspx

Healthy Active Australia
www.healthyactive.gov.au/

Organizations

British Nutrition Foundation
High Holburn House
52-54 High Holburn
London WC1V 6RQ
Tel:020 7404 6504   Fax:020 7404 6747
E-mail: postbox@nutrition.org.uk
Website: www.nutrition.org.uk

Food Standards Agency
Aviation House
125 Kingsway
London WC2B 6NH
Tel: 020 7276 8000
Website: www.food.gov.uk

Index